SARPEDON
a play by
Gregory Corso

D1600795

TOUGH POETS PRESS

CONTENTS

EDITOR'S INTRODUCTION

Readers who have ventured this deeply into the bibliography of Gregory Corso (1930–2001) are probably already aware of his prominence among post-World War II poets, as well as familiar with his close personal and professional associations with the other three writers — Jack Kerouac, Allen Ginsberg, and William Burroughs — credited with launching and popularizing the Beat movement in American literature in the late 1950s. Not so well known is that, in addition to several volumes of poetry, Corso also wrote a novel (*The American Express*, Olympia Press, 1961) and several plays, the first of which was *Sarpedon*. "A great funny *Prometheus Unbound* ... all in metre and rhyme,"[1] as Corso himself described it, *Sarpedon* was one of three plays he wrote while living covertly on the campus of Harvard University between 1954 and 1955.

Corso was brought to Cambridge by Violet "Bunny" Lang, a Boston socialite, poet, playwright, and co-founder of The Poets' Theatre, shortly after their meeting in Allen Ginsberg's New York City apartment. Recognizing Corso's potential and wishing to assist him as he developed his poetic voice, she set him up in a $5-a-week room at 12 Ash St. Place near Harvard Square, as well as provided him with a small income for sweeping up at the theater. When the City of Cambridge informed the house's owner that he could not legally rent out rooms, Lang arranged for Corso to share space in Harvard's Eliot House with future novelist Peter Sourian and his roommates, Paul Grand and Bobby Sedgwick, brother of actress, model, and Andy Warhol "superstar" Edie Sedgwick.

Bunny Lang's support of Corso may not have been purely altruistic. According to Nora Sayle, a Radcliffe undergraduate and member of The Poets' Theatre at the time, "planting Corso in Cambridge was probably a deliberate act of sedition. No one at Harvard — not even the New Yorkers — had met anyone like him, and [Lang] took him to starchy gatherings and urged him to be insolent."[2] She further noted that "Sourian was sure that Bunny had plucked Corso from Greenwich Village to flout the Cantabrigian principles that she herself was eager to derail."[3]

Regardless of Lang's true rationale behind bringing Corso to Cambridge, the time he spent at Harvard proved to be invaluable to his career. The university's two literary magazines, the *Harvard Advocate* and *i.e., the Cambridge Review*, were first to publish his poetry; and his first collection, The *Vestal Lady on Brattle and Other Poems*, was published in 1955 by Harvard undergrad Richard Brukenfeld with funds contributed by fellow students.

Unless you count Corso's 1978 recorded reading of *Sarpedon* as part of a guest lecture at the Naropa Institute[4] (now Naropa University) in Boulder, Colorado, only one of the three plays he wrote at Harvard was ever performed and published. The New Theatre Workshop's April 28, 1955 performance of *In This Hung-Up Age* was considered "a minor triumph" by a *Harvard Crimson* reviewer who wrote that "The language of his characters is fast, vigorous, and funny, and the denouement is grotesquely original." and "Its humor and its design are blunt; it elicits spontaneous enthusiasm."[5] The play was first published in 1962 as *In This Hung-Up: A One-Act Farce Written in 1954* in the literary magazine *Encounter*, and subsequently reprinted in *New Directions in Prose and Poetry 18* (1964) and *The Kenning Anthology of Poets Theater 1945–1985* (2010).

There is little historical documentation of *The Death of a Beautiful Boy*, the third play Corso wrote at this time. In a 1956 letter to Randall Jarrell, then Consultant in Poetry to the U.S. Library of Congress, Corso described it as "all about a Shelleyan youngster caught in the throes of N.Y.C."[6] Apparently, Corso was not too pleased with this early work, effectively disowning it a few years later. His 1968 handwritten note on the 108-page typescript of the play held in the Special Collections Library at Stony Brook University reads as follows:

> *This is the only extant copy of final play — by me,*
> *Gregory Corso — I do not wish any of this to be*
> *published or performed while I live & die — as I*
> *consider this a terrible yet soul-draining effort —*

Sarpedon, on the other hand, was no such failure in Corso's opinion. Referring to the play in a 1959 letter to New Directions publisher James Laughlin, he boasted "I can even do that!"[7]

Corso never professed to be a Greek scholar but this brilliant yet little-known work clearly demonstrates the depth of his mastery of classical literature, no doubt picked up from auditing Harvard lectures as well as from the extensive reading he did in the Clinton State Prison library in Dannemora, New York, while serving a three-year sentence for theft. What makes it all the more significant is that, despite the ancient subject matter, his verse is infused with the street slang and Beat vernacular of the time in which it was written, and portends the irreverent humor that would become a hallmark of much of his later work.

Rick Schober

* * * * * * *

The punctuation, line breaks, and handwritten edits from Corso's original 1954 typescript of *Sarpedon* have been preserved in this publication. Obvious misspellings have been corrected. Because the Greek and English alphabets are substantially different, there are various accepted spellings of proper names in *The Iliad*. Based on his use of "-os" at the end of several characters' names, it is likely that Corso was most familiar with Richmond Lattimore's 1951 translation, *The Iliad of Homer* (University of Chicago Press).

CORSO'S INTRODUCTION TO HIS 1978 READING

From Gregory Corso's prefatory comments on his reading of
Sarpedon *at the Naropa Institute, July 20, 1978.*[1]

Anybody know Sarpedon? Oh, okay. Sarpedon was known in America about four years ago [1974] by the calyx krater[2] made by Euphronios 5 B.C. Sarpedon is dead, you see. It's the death of Sarpedon. Between him is Hypnos and Thanatos. Death and Sleep. In 1954 I wrote it — 24 years ago — that's when I first hit Harvard. Mr. Finley,[3] a great Greek scholar, was running Eliot House and I was told by one of his TAs, if I could write a Greek play I could stay at Eliot House. I did it overnight.[4] Now the way you do it, you take the Homeric hit like Aeschylus, Sophocles, Euripides. They all played on it. So I played on this ballgame.

Front side of the Euphronius Krater depicting Sarpedon's body carried by Hypnos and Thanatos while Hermes watches. (Photo by Jaime Ardiles-Arce)

Sarpedon is the son of Europa and Zeus.[5] Remember the painting of Titian and Rubens? Over the water the bull is taking the woman? Well, he's the son. Okay. He's on the side of the Trojans. Remember the water. Poseidon, the god of the water, is for the Trojans. Zeus, the daddy of the skies. Hades, the third brother, the underworld. Okay, this is how I created it.

Being they're gonna have their war, Hades gets all the dead on the fields of Troy. Now, remember what I told you that's on this big calyx krater that made noise four years ago in New York in the Metropolitan. They ripped it off. They paid two mill for it.[6] Okay.

"Sar-*PEE*-don." Not saltpeter. I could say "*SAR*-pe-don" but my rhyme goes "Sar-*PEE*-don." All right.

"... a play, my first, about 12 pages, *Sarpedon*, 1954, in verse. [It] was an attempt to replicate Euripides, though the whole shot be an original. Like the great Greek masters, I took off where Homer left an opening (like Euripides did with the fate of Agamemnon). My opening was found in the *Iliad*. Sarpedon, son of Zeus and Europa, died on the fields of Troy, and Homer had him sent up to Olympus with no complaint from Hades, who got all the others what died there. Thus I have Hades complain, demanding from his brother Zeus, the dead, all the dead, from said fields."

From Corso's October 25, 1978, letter to New Directions publisher James Laughlin, discussing the possibility of Lawrence Ferlinghetti publishing a collection of his plays.

Source: Corso, Gregory, and Bill Morgan, Ed.. *An Accidental Autobiography: The Selected Letters of Gregory Corso.* (New York: New Directions, 2003): 405–406.

SARPEDON

It is agreed. There will be war.
Zeus the Greeks.
Poseidon the Trojans.
And Hades the Dead.

The entrance of the Underworld. In the dim misty light of dawn,
the Roll Caller, standing beside Charon,[1] is calling the names of
the new dead. Hades, checking the dead that file past him, stands
to the left of Charon.

    ROLL CALLER
Orsilochos, Ormenos, Daitor, Chromios.
Come on, move along. Melanippos,
Lycophontes, Archeptolemos.[2]

    CHARON
That does it.

    ROLL CALLER
I counted 70.

    CHARON
That's correct. Let's be off.

    HADES
Hey, wait! 71.
My list has it 71.

    CHARON
You want us to make a recount?

HADES
I know who's missing.
Sarpedon. Where is he? He's due.

CHARON
True.

HADES
Well ... where is he?

CHARON
Don't ask me.

HADES
What do you mean, 'don't ask me'?
Who am I supposed to ask?

CHARON
I don't like the tone of your voice.

HADES
Fool! You expect me to rejoice?
Sarpedon is mine now that's he's dead.

CHARON
I bring you all the dead I get
— in and out of season.
Mine's a lousy job. I get all wet.
Yet you curse me for not bringing Sarpedon.
Look at me all smelly and drippy with rot;
that's the thanks I get joining your miserable lot.
You think because you gave me a silver oar
for last Zeusmas I am indebted to you,
well you're mistaken;
if you can chew the ham you can fry the bacon.

HADES
Keep Menelaus's tags out of this.[3]

CHARON
I warn you Hades if you keep tormenting me
treating me like a delivery boy
I'll cease to bring the dead to be
from the gory fields of Troy.

HADES
Charon, all I want is my due.
Sarpedon is mine and that's true.

CHARON
True or no, you insulted me.
I never used tags used by others.
You have no right to say I do.
Do you doubt I created:
Men may be gods but they'll never be mothers?

HADES
Every day you bring me cowards and spies
who have fallen on the fields of Troy,
but now that a son of Zeus by Patroclus[4] dies
— I thought surely he'd be on today's envoy.

CHARON
Whoever's on the shore
I pick up. That's my job, no more.
Who they be, swineherds or sons of Zeus, I care not.
Dead they're all the same or have you forgot?

HADES
Sarpedon is something special.
He's unlike the common mortal.
His mother was Europa
and his father, a bull.

CHARON
I know the story.

HADES
Then I want Sarpedon!

CHARON
There were 70 on shore.
Only 70 — no more.
Ah yes, Hephaestus was there.
He made a cup for you — here.

HADES
A cup? For me? What did he say?

CHARON
Happy birthday.

HADES
It is my birthday. Good old Hephaestus!

ROLL CALLER
Hadn't we better get a move on?

CHARON
Yes.

HADES
No! No one leaves! Not until
I find out what became of Sarpedon.
You're up to something Charon.
I warn you, be careful
or you'll be sorry.

CHARON
How's this? Sorry?
Who's going to make me sorry?

HADES
No one. All I want ...

CHARON
How are you going to make me sorry?

HADES
If I don't get Sarpedon
you'll soon see how.

CHARON
Well, just for that Sarpedon you'll never see.
I'll let him stand on the shore
no matter how much you or he implore.
He'll stay there! In the black mist he'll toss!
And I dare him defy me and swim across!
I'll teach you to threaten me
you gloomy husband to Persephone.

HADES
I didn't mean to threaten you.
O I am the saddest of the gods!
Poseidon has his earthquakes
and Zeus his lightning rods
and I — I have you.
And what do you do?
Treat me as you would the dead
and call me gloomy to the wife I wed.

CHARON
All right, all right, stop cryin'.
I can't bear to hear those tears of iron.

EXIT CHARON AND ROLL CALLER

HADES
Fish head! Wait, someday I'll show him
damn! If only the dead were able to swim!

ENTER PERSEPHONE

PERSEPHONE
What are you mumbling about?

HADES
Shhh must you shout?
What will the guards think?
O if only his boat would sink!

PERSEPHONE
Charon? Ha! What would you do without Charon?
You pray he drowns? Ha! Go, pray on.
Surely the dead will swim across that ink.
And I don't give a fig for what the guards think.
I'm mistress here, aye, Queen! and I do as I please.

HADES
All right. Enough! Geez —
must everybody pounce on me like this?
First it's Sarpedon I miss
then Charon with his disrespect
and now you, what next to expect?
And why haven't you given the newly dead their linen?
Look at them hanging around waiting to be fed.
Go, console them, entertain them,
play them my latest requiem.

PERSEPHONE
Who are you married to anyway
me or the dead?
You hardly notice me anymore,
not even in bed.

HADES
A god finds joy in many things
the joys of the bed are all right
but a god knows greater things
such as counting bones in the night.

PERSEPHONE
Great joy.

HADES
Besides, there's much to be done;
as of now there's Sarpedon.

PERSEPHONE
What a lovely cup!
Is it for me? From my mother?

HADES
Hands off! Hephaestus gave it to me
for my birthday; it's mine.
But what a birthday! I'm so unhappy!
I wanted him so terribly much.
Among mortal men he's Zeus' proudest son.
I'm sick of champion bowmen
spies cowards and such.
That's all I've been getting!
My kingdom's become a rat nest!
Well I'll get him I swear I'll not rest!

PERSEPHONE
You didn't even notice my new hair-do.

HADES
Why should I? Besides, I don't care to.
Did you remember my birthday?

PERSEPHONE
You're a cold god, Hades.

ENTER ORMENOS

ORMENOS
Hey, where are all the ladies?

HADES
Guards! Get this ass out of here!

PERSEPHONE
Look, there's Charon!

HADES
O Charon you brought Sarpedon!

CHARON
No — Hector.

PERSEPHONE
O he's much better than Sarpedon!

CHARON
The best!

HECTOR
Good but not good enough, that's me.
Prince of Troy! Joy to Andromache!
Much feared was I, this the Argives know.
See my sword? See the red blood glow!
Many battles this sword for me has won.

HADES
Take him back!

CHARON
What?

HADES
I want Sarpedon!

CHARON
Can't be done.

HECTOR
Ah Persephone!
You are as I imagined you too be,
are you not Aphrodite?

PERSEPHONE
O sweetest of husbands
do let Hector stay.

HADES
No! I don't trust that Priam family.
Wife-stealers, that's what they are, all of them![5]

PERSEPHONE
O don't be silly
who would want to steal me?

CHARON
It's getting so I don't like coming here anymore.
I thought I was doing you a favor by bringing Hector.
I've a good mind to go and complain to Zeus!
Damn it, I will!

EXIT CHARON

HADES
What do I care of Zeus?
I own my own religion!
Go ahead, go tell him,
you stool-pigeon!

The following day, Hermes is sent to Hades by Zeus.

HERMES
Okay, what's up? Zeus sent me.
He doesn't like to see Charon upset.
What did you do to him? No mind.
Zeus wants to know what's troubling you.
Say what you have to say, and let things be done.

HADES

Tell him I didn't get Sarpedon.
Tell him it was agreed that my share of the war
was to have all the dead. And Sarpedon is dead!
Tell him if I don't get Sarpedon I'll close my doors!
Tell him the dead will pile up!
Tell him – *what*? What have you there?

HERMES

Where?

HADES

There! Behind your back.
Ah! I caught you!
O Zeus is this how you go about finding what's up?
This pest tried to steal Hephaestus's cup!
Thief! Thief! Give it back!

HERMES

Easy, man.
I didn't steal it
I only wanted to feel it.
Everybody's always accusing me.
I'm your guest;
you're supposed to be amusing me.

HADES

Don't give me that!
I know your sob stories.
You're a thief through and through.
As soon as you were born
you stole Hyperion's cows;[6]
now tell me that's not true.

HERMES

Please, don't bug me about my youth.

HADES

It's the truth, isn't it? The truth!

HERMES

Man, you're nowhere.
No wonder poor Charon was in such despair.

EXIT HERMES

HADES

Guard!

GUARD

Good thing you called. The dead,
there's unrest; they want to be fed.

HADES

My wife does nothing; work is piling up.
The dead are hungry and the tables bare.
Here hide this cup
else it end in the sink
with the rest of the silverware.

GUARD

Should I go get your wife?

HADES

Bah! Let her be.
I've got to do something.
Can't let them get away with this.
Sarpedon! Sarpedon! Sarpedon!

GUARD

True. Sarpedon is a painful worry.
And there are things to think about
and things to forget.
But shouldn't something be done?
The dead are very hungry, especially Dolon.
He screams the loudest. I fear revolt.

HADES
What? Dolon! That disgusting spy! Revolt!
Fetch him at once!
I'll show him who's who down here.

EXIT GUARD

ENTER GUARD WITH DOLON

DOLON
Ah Hades most illustrious god
I come on behalf of my fellow dead;
as their spokesman, we demand ...

HADES
Shut up! How dare you?
You come because I have ordered it so!
Spy! Miscreant!
Hector is here;
he has not forgotten how you bungled your mission.
Achilles horses, indeed![7]
Oxen is too good for you, incompetent ass!

DOLON
Hector forgives,
and that's more one could say for you.

HADES
O that Odysseus and Diomedes had left
your carcass to rot in the sun!

DOLON
Rumor has it you'll not get Sarpedon.
Rumor has it he's in Elysium.

VOICES OF THE DEAD
Food! Clean cerements![8] New requiems! Rusty nails!

HADES

Persephone! Persephone!

GUARD

Don't expect her to come.
She and Hector are a twosome.
Together they pluck dead flowers
and watch the little bats make love,
and sometimes they watch for hours
like two fingers in a one-finger glove.

HADES

I knew it! Asphodels!⁹ I knew he'd steal her!
O Zeus, you cow-eater! I'll make you pay!
It's all your fault! I won't be treated this way!
Isn't your wife enough? Must you have mine too?
I know you've taken Hector's form! Bastard!
Rape artist! You can't fool me!
How would you like it if somebody raped your wife?
It could happen; it could just happen!
And I'm the one to do it too.

DOLON

This bickering over ladies
ain't gonna feed the dead, Hades.

HADES

Away! Leave me alone.
I am the saddest of gods.
No one loves me.
No one sacrifices anything to me.
All they do is cheat! Hermes steals my cup,
Charon doesn't bring me Sarpedon,
and that cow-eater rapes my wife!

GUARD

Why don't you go up
and have it out with him?

HADES
I'll just do that!
Get me a bat.

GUARD
The bats are making love.

HADES
Hang it! I'll go without one.

Olympus. Hades is standing before Zeus who is in a great hurry.

HADES
Here you are, don't deny what you've done!
You raped my wife and stole Sarpedon!

ZEUS
Can't talk now, got to run.
20 cows in Ethiopia;
I'm starved. Come again.
Sarpedon? See Europa.
Sorry, can't introduce her.

EXIT ZEUS

HADES
How he treats me! Am I not as powerful as he?
Ah, there's his wife. I'll show him!
Just a little closer and then I'll pounce on her.

He pounces on who he thinks to be Hera but who is actually
Aphrodite.

APHRODITE
Hel ———— p!

ENTER HEPHAESTUS

HEPHAESTUS
O Hades is this the thanks I get?
This is the worst seduction of my wife yet!
And after I spent two months on that cup for you.

HADES
O dear
It was an error
I had no idea
I thought it was Hera.

APHRODITE
I'm not to blame this time, Hephaestus.
Remember when Ares — and what you did to us?[10]

HEPHAESTUS
I want my cup back!

HADES
But … but …

HEPHAESTUS
And my fire! You'll get no more heat from me!

Back in his dark kingdom Hades sits dejected on his throne.

VOICES OF THE DEAD
Heat! Food! Warmer cerements!

DOLON
Hades, the dead need heat!

HADES
What about me?
Look at my feet, how blue!
I've never been so cold!
What am I to do?

DOLON

If there's no fire
couldn't we have food at least?
Nothing much, just some rusty wire
even oily rags will do.
We don't expect a feast,
and I'm sorry your feet are blue.

GUARD

Hades, the Styx has turned to ice!

DOLON

Even bent nails will suffice.

GUARD

Charon says he not going to skate across.

DOLON

It isn't as if we were asking for steak.

ENTER PERSEPHONE

PERSEPHONE

What is this I hear — Aphrodite?
Well! from now on
don't expect me to keep things tidy.

DOLON

Madam, we are cold.

PERSEPHONE

Indeed the weather is not pleasing.
I guess something should be done.
My dead flowers are freezing
— who's this, Sarpedon?

DOLON

I am Dolon, spokesman for the dead.
We need food and heat and cerements.

ENTER HERMES

HERMES
I've come for Hephaestus's cup.
I didn't think you had in in you. How was it?

HADES
How was what?

HERMES
Aw, come off it man, you know what I mean.
Aphrodite. I take my hat off to you,
she's the immortal end.

HADES
It was a mistake, a terrible mistake!

HERMES
Sure, man, sure.

HADES
Leave me alone you degenerate.

DOLON
Food! Heat!

HADES
A mistake! A mistake!

PERSEPHONE
Look at him brag!

VOICES OF THE DEAD
Give us back life!

END

NOTES

EDITOR'S INTRODUCTION

1. Corso, Gregory, and Bill Morgan, Ed.. *An Accidental Autobiography: The Selected Letters of Gregory Corso.* (New York: New Directions, 2003): 200.

2. Sayre, Nora. "The Poets' Theatre: A Memoir of the Fifties". *Grand Street,* Vol. 3 No. 3. (New York: Grand Street Publications, 1984): 102.

3. Ibid., 103.

4. Corso, Gregory. "Socratic Poetry Rap 7/20/1978." *JKS Audio Collection.* (Boulder, Colorado: Naropa University Archives, 1978): <http://cdm16621. contentdm.oclc.org/cdm/ref/collection/p16621coll1/id/2203>.

5. Pope, John A. "New Theatre Workshops at Agassiz." *Harvard Crimson.* (Cambridge: April 30, 1955).

6. Corso, Gregory, and Bill Morgan, Ed.. *An Accidental Autobiography: The Selected Letters of Gregory Corso.* (New York: New Directions, 2003): 16.

7. Ibid., 200.

AUTHOR'S INTRODUCTION

1. Corso, Gregory. "Socratic Poetry Rap 7/20/1978." *JKS Audio Collection.* (Boulder, Colorado: Naropa University Archives, 1978): <http://cdm16621. contentdm.oclc.org/cdm/ref/collection/p16621coll1/id/2203>.

2. A large vase, shaped like the calyx of a flower, typically used in ancient Greece for mixing water and wine. The specific krater to which Corso referred is known as the Euphronios Krater or Sarpedon Krater. Created around 515 BC, it depicts on one side the death of Sarpedon in the Trojan War. It is the only complete example of the surviving 27 vases painted by the renowned Euphronios (circa 535–470 BC).

3. John H. Finley Jr. (1904–1995), classics professor and Harvard faculty member from 1933 to 1976, Master of Eliot House from 1941 to 1968.

4. This is possibly a fabrication on Corso's part, according to Dick Brukenfeld, Harvard Class of 1955 and publisher of Corso's *The Vestal Lady on Brattle and Other Poems.* "I have no recollection of the play, and Gregory's explanation is convincing at first sight. But my guess is that he didn't write it when he first hit Harvard. My understanding is that Finley and the other Eliot House officials didn't know of his presence at Eliot House at first. It

took a while for his existence as a stowaway there to be known. It makes more sense that after he was established there and known as an avid-for-knowledge poet, one of Finley's assistants would give him the challenge of writing a Greek play in order to stay." (Source: Dick Brukenfeld email, May 23, 2015.)

5. The Sarpedon featured in *The Iliad* is actually the son of Zeus and Laodameia, not the son of Zeus and Europa. Lines 198 and 199 from Book VI of *The Iliad* confirm this: "Laodameia lay in love beside Zeus of the counsels / and bore him godlike Sarpedon of the brazen helmet." (Source: Richmond Lattimore's 1951 translation.) In Greek mythology, there are three different characters named Sarpedon, the third being a son of Poseidon.

6. The krater was reportedly looted from an Etruscan tomb in central Italy in December 1971 by illegal excavators and sold for $1.2 million to the Metropolitan Museum of Art where it remained in its collection from 1972 to 2008. It was returned to Italy under an agreement negotiated in February 2006 and is now in the collection of the National Etruscan Museum in Rome.

SARPEDON

1. The ferryman of Hades who carried the souls of the newly deceased across the rivers Styx and Acheron that divided the world of the living from the world of the dead.

2. Trojan warriors killed by the Greek archer Teucer (Tuekros) in Book VIII of *The Iliad*.

3. Menelaus, king of Sparta, was the husband of Helen. She was abducted by Paris, prince of Troy, although, according to some accounts, she fell in love with Paris and left willingly. The Greeks' expedition to rescue Helen from Paris is the mythological basis for the Trojan War. It would be reasonable to assume that Corso used the word "tags" here as an accepted shortened form of "taglines," a word that first came into usage in the mid-1930s, meaning "frequently repeated quotations or characteristic catchphrases." However, an exhaustive search of translated ancient Greek texts revealed no mention of either ham or bacon in any expression attributed to Menelaus.

4. Patroclus killed Sarpedon in Book XVI of *The Iliad*.

5. Both Paris (see note 3 above) and Hector were sons of Priam, king of Troy during the Trojan War.

6. In the play *Ichneutae* by Sophocles (circa 497–406 BC), newborn Hermes steals Apollo's cattle. Hyperion's herd of golden cattle are mentioned in *The Odyssey*. They are slaughtered by Odysseus's men and Hyperion has Zeus kill them in retribution.

7. Hector offered Dolon the horses and chariot of Achilles as a reward for spying on the Greeks. Dolon was captured by Odysseus and Diomedes and, in exchange for his life, revealed the location of some of his Trojan allies. He was decapitated by Diomedes regardless.

8. Burial garments made from wax-coated cloth.

9. Flowers often associated in literature with the ancient Greek underworld.

10. Aphrodite had countless lovers, both divine and mortal, including Ares, the god of war. Informed by Helios of his wife's adulterous affair with Ares, Hephaestus took revenge on the lovers by fashioning an invisible and unbreakable net of chains, trapping them together, and exposing them to the ridicule of the other gods at Mt. Olympus. (*The Odyssey*, Book VIII)

ACKNOWLEDGMENTS

I would like to express my gratitiude to the following for their information, materials, permissions, and/or encouragement, without which this little book may never have seen the light of day: Sheri Langerman-Baird, Peter Hale of the Allen Ginsberg LLC, George Scrivani, Dick Brukenfeld, Ronna Johnson, Bill Morgan, Kaye McDonough, Michael Skau, the Allen Ginsberg Library and Archives at Naropa University, the Frank Melville, Jr. Memorial Library at Stony Brook University, and the Morgan Library & Museum.

Also, I would like to thank the following for their generous financial support which helped to defray some of the book's production costs: Theo Alpert, Paul E. Bach, Jr., Nate Ballard, Timothy Edward Barnes, Beatdom Literary Journal, Cameron Bennett, Dan Buckle, John Burns, Jared A. Carnie, Walter F. Croft, Livingston Conant, Tyler Crumrine, David Depestel, Travis DeSilva, V.J. Eaton, John Feins, Leo Fitz-James Gray, James A. Houlahan, Haya K, Larry Kerschner, Josh Mahler, Richard Marsh, Tim McAllister, Alexander McLean, Mark S. Mitchell, Moe (Sigma Alpha Mu Beta Epsilon Chapter UMass '81), Thurston Moore, William Nesbitt, Carl Orend, Poems-For-All, Dustin Rimmey, Walter Raubicheck, Matthew J. Rogers, bhikkhu Japhy Ryder, Frank V. Saltarelli, Brant Shapiro, t kilgore splake, David Starner, Pamela Twining, and Tim Wheatley.

CPSIA information can be obtained
at www.ICGtesting.com
Printed in the USA
LVOW10s1226310717
543261LV00025B/979/P